THE UNIVERSE WITHIN:

CRACKING THE CODE TO YOUR INNER POWER

MEERA

The Universe Within: Cracking the Code to Your Inner Power

By

Meera

Copyright© Meera 2023

Originally Published in India

ISBN: 978-93-95773-55-3

Published by RIGI PUBLICATION
Printer: RIGI PRINTERS

777, Street no.9, Krishna Nagar

Khanna-141401 (Punjab), India

Website: www.rigipublication.com

Email: info@rigipublication.com

Phone: +91-9357710014, +91-9465468291

Preface

"The Universe Within: Cracking the Code to Your Inner Power" is a transformative guide that leads readers on a profound journey of self-discovery and empowerment. This captivating book delves into the essence of inner power and explores the untapped potential that lies dormant within each individual. As readers venture further, they uncover the interconnectedness between the universe and their inner selves, awakening to the cosmic energy that resides within.

The chapters of this enlightening book serve as stepping stones towards self-discovery, starting with nurturing self-awareness and harnessing the power of introspection. Readers learn to tap into their inner reservoir of strength, cultivating resilience to overcome challenges and adversities.

The book reveals the art of aligning with cosmic energy, harmonizing one's energy with the universal flow to harness the power of alignment for manifestation. By activating their inner potential and unleashing unique gifts and talents, readers are empowered to live a purposeful and fulfilling life.

The cosmic connection is explored in-depth, as readers deepen their connection to the universal intelligence and learn to trust their intuition, accessing divine guidance along their path.

The power of intention and visualization are harnessed to manifest desires, aligning personal intentions with the greater cosmic plan. Embracing the journey of self-love and acceptance, readers recognize the foundation of inner power and embrace their inherent worth.

As readers integrate inner power into their daily lives, the book inspires them to apply these principles to relationships, career, and personal growth, ultimately leading to a lifestyle that reflects their true inner power and authenticity.

In the conclusion, readers are encouraged to embrace their cosmic potential fully, unlocking a life of purpose, connection, and profound fulfillment. "The Universe Within" serves as a guiding light, illuminating the path towards unlocking the true power that resides within, ultimately transforming lives and fostering a deeper connection with the vast cosmos.

Introduction: Embarking on the Journey Within

Embarking on the Journey Within is a transformative exploration that beckons us to venture into the uncharted territories of our inner selves. It is an invitation to embark on a quest of self-discovery, a pilgrimage to unearth the hidden treasures of our souls. In a fast-paced world teeming with external distractions, this journey calls us to turn inward, to listen to the whispers of our hearts, and to connect with the essence of who we truly are.

The journey within is not a mere physical endeavor, but a profound odyssey of the mind, heart, and spirit. It is a pilgrimage that leads us through the landscapes of our emotions, thoughts, and beliefs, unveiling the intricate tapestry of our inner worlds. Along the way, we encounter the depths of our fears and insecurities, as well as the heights of our dreams and aspirations.

Yet, in this sacred exploration, we find not just our vulnerabilities but also our boundless resilience. As we traverse the landscapes of our souls, we cultivate a deeper understanding of ourselves and our place in the universe. We come to realize that our stories are interwoven with the larger tapestry of humanity, and our journey is intimately connected with the journeys of others.

This pilgrimage of self-discovery demands courage, vulnerability, and a willingness to confront the shadows within. It beckons us to release the burdens we carry and to embrace the light that resides in our hearts. In the depths of our souls, we find the wellspring of wisdom, love, and inner power that can guide us through life's trials and triumphs.

With each step on this transformative journey, we gain clarity, insight, and a deeper sense of purpose. We unearth the hidden gems of our unique gifts and talents, which have long awaited recognition and expression. As we delve into the depths of our being, we come to understand that the journey within is not a destination but a continuous evolution, a never-ending process of growth and self-awareness.

As we embark on the journey within, we recognize that we are not alone but part of a larger cosmic dance. The universe conspires in our favor, guiding us, supporting us, and showering us with blessings. This pilgrimage is a sacred communion with our own souls and the universe that surrounds us.

May this journey within be a source of inspiration and transformation, leading us to embrace the richness of our inner worlds and the limitless potential that resides within. Let us open our hearts to the whispers of our souls and embark on this sacred pilgrimage, where we find the true essence of our being and unlock the profound treasures of our inner selves.

Embarking on the Journey Within is a transformative exploration that beckons us to venture into the uncharted territories of our inner selves. It is an invitation to embark on a quest of self-discovery, a pilgrimage to unearth the hidden treasures of our souls. In a fast-paced world teeming with external distractions, this journey calls us to turn inward, to listen to the whispers of our hearts, and to connect with the essence of who we truly are.

The journey within is not a mere physical endeavor, but a profound odyssey of the mind, heart, and spirit. It is a pilgrimage that leads us through the landscapes of our emotions, thoughts, and beliefs, unveiling the intricate tapestry of our inner worlds. Along the way, we encounter the depths of our fears and insecurities, as well as the heights of our dreams and aspirations.

Yet, in this sacred exploration, we find not just our vulnerabilities but also our boundless resilience. As we traverse the landscapes of our souls, we cultivate a deeper understanding of ourselves and our place in the universe. We come to realize that our stories are interwoven with the larger tapestry of humanity, and our journey is intimately connected with the journeys of others.

This pilgrimage of self-discovery demands courage, vulnerability, and a willingness to confront the shadows within. It beckons us to release the burdens we carry and to embrace the light that resides in our hearts. In the depths of our souls, we find the wellspring of wisdom, love, and inner power that can guide us through life's trials and triumphs.

With each step on this transformative journey, we gain clarity, insight, and a deeper sense of purpose. We unearth the hidden gems of our unique gifts and talents, which have long awaited recognition and expression. As we delve into the depths of our being, we come to understand that the journey within is not a destination but a continuous evolution, a never-ending process of growth and self-awareness.

As we embark on the journey within, we recognize that we are not alone but part of a larger cosmic dance. The universe conspires in our favor, guiding us, supporting us, and showering us with blessings. This pilgrimage is a sacred communion with our own souls and the universe that surrounds us.

May this journey within be a source of inspiration and transformation, leading us to embrace the richness of our inner worlds and the limitless potential that resides within. Let us open our hearts to the whispers of our souls and embark on this sacred pilgrimage, where we find the true essence of our being and unlock the profound treasures of our inner Selves.

THE UNIVERSE WITHIN: CRACKING THE CODE TO YOUR INNER POWER

- MEERA

INDEX

Chapter 1
The Essence of Inner Power

In this pivotal chapter, we embark on a profound exploration of the very core of our being - the essence of inner power. We delve into the concept of inner power, understanding its nature and significance in shaping our lives. By unraveling the untapped potential within, we come to realize that true strength is not about external dominance, but the ability to harness our thoughts, emotions, and beliefs to manifest positive change.

Through introspection and self-awareness, we gain deeper insights into our unique strengths and weaknesses, recognizing the power that lies dormant within us. As we navigate through the landscapes of our inner selves, we confront the barriers that have held us back, embracing vulnerability and courage to break free from self-imposed limitations.

By embracing the essence of inner power, we foster a profound sense of purpose and clarity of thought. This newfound understanding empowers us to navigate life's challenges with resilience and grace. As we recognize the interconnectedness between our inner selves and the universe, we begin to realize that our actions have far-reaching impacts beyond ourselves.

In the journey of self-discovery, we uncover the keys to unlocking the boundless potential within, paving the way for personal growth and fulfillment. With each revelation, we learn that inner power is not a finite resource, but an infinite wellspring of strength and wisdom waiting to be tapped into.

By embracing the essence of inner power, we set the stage for a transformative and empowering journey that leads us towards self-mastery and a deeper connection with our true selves. This chapter lays the foundation for the exploration of our cosmic potential, inspiring us to unlock the door to our inner power and embrace the remarkable journey that lies ahead.

- *Understanding the concept of inner power*

Understanding the concept of inner power is the key to unlocking our true potential and living a fulfilling life. Inner power is not about external control or dominance over others; rather, it is the profound ability to harness the strength, wisdom, and resilience that reside within ourselves.

At its core, inner power is rooted in self-awareness and self-belief. It is the recognition of our unique strengths, talents, and abilities, as well as an acceptance of our vulnerabilities and limitations. Embracing both aspects of ourselves allows us to cultivate a sense of authenticity and genuine confidence.

Inner power is not about suppressing emotions or denying vulnerabilities; instead, it involves acknowledging and embracing them as part of our human experience. By developing a deep understanding of our thoughts, emotions, and beliefs, we gain insight into what drives our actions and reactions.

With this self-awareness, we can make conscious choices and align our actions with our core values and aspirations. Inner power empowers us to take responsibility for our lives, embracing the freedom to shape our own destinies.

Furthermore, inner power is closely intertwined with resilience. It is the ability to bounce back from setbacks, learn from failures, and grow stronger in the face of challenges. By nurturing inner power, we cultivate a sense of adaptability and perseverance, which are essential qualities on the path to success and fulfillment.

Inner power also extends to our relationships with others and the world around us. When we are grounded in our inner strength, we are less influenced by external circumstances and opinions. Instead, we can approach interactions with empathy, compassion, and understanding.

In essence, understanding and harnessing our inner power is a transformative journey of self-discovery. It is an ongoing process that involves introspection, self-acceptance, and continuous growth. By embracing our inner power, we step into our authenticity and create a positive impact on ourselves and the world. It empowers us to lead lives of purpose, resilience, and profound fulfillment.

- *Exploring the untapped potential within*

Exploring the untapped potential within is an awe-inspiring journey of self-discovery, inviting us to delve into the depths of our being to unearth the dormant capabilities and hidden treasures that reside within us. It is an exploration of the vast and boundless reservoir of untapped potential that has yet to be fully realized.

This journey starts with a willingness to look beyond our comfort zones and embrace vulnerability. As we open ourselves up to new possibilities, we begin to unravel the layers of self-imposed limitations and beliefs that have held us back from reaching our full potential.

By exploring the untapped potential within, we gain insight into our unique strengths, talents, and passions. We come to understand that there is a wellspring of creativity, resilience, and wisdom waiting to be harnessed for our personal growth and transformation.

This journey involves confronting our fears and doubts, as well as embracing failure as a stepping stone towards growth. As we push past our perceived boundaries, we discover the exhilarating feeling of pushing the limits of what we once thought was possible.

Exploring the untapped potential within is not a one-time event, but an ongoing process of self-discovery and self-improvement. It requires continuous reflection, self-awareness, and a willingness to learn from every experience.

As we tap into our untapped potential, we gain the courage to pursue our dreams and aspirations, knowing that we have the power to shape our own destinies. This journey is an empowering experience that fuels us with motivation and a sense of purpose, as we realize that our potential is truly limitless.

In this exploration, we connect with our authentic selves and embrace the uniqueness of who we are. We recognize that our journey is different from anyone else's, and that our untapped potential holds the key to unlocking a life of fulfillment, success, and genuine happiness.

Embarking on the journey to explore the untapped potential within is an act of self-love and self-empowerment. It is an acknowledgement of our inherent worth and the understanding that we are capable of achieving greatness.

With each step on this transformative journey, we shed the limitations that have held us back and embrace the freedom to reach new heights. As we explore the untapped potential within, we come to understand that it is not only a journey of self-discovery but also a path to self-actualization, leading us to become the best versions of ourselves.

Chapter 2
Unveiling the Universe Within

In this profound chapter, we embark on a journey of self-discovery and interconnectedness, as we unveil the vast universe that resides within each of us. We come to understand that our inner selves are intricately connected to the grand cosmos, and this realization opens the door to profound transformation and enlightenment.

Example 1: The Microcosm and the Macrocosm

Just as the universe is vast and expansive, so too is the universe within us. Science and spirituality both point to the idea that we are composed of stardust and interconnected with the cosmos. The elements that make up our bodies are the same elements found in the stars. This beautiful connection reminds us that we are not separate from the universe but an integral part of it. By recognizing this unity, we can tap into the cosmic energy that flows through us, awakening to the profound wisdom and power that lies within.

Example 2: The Power of Mindfulness and Introspection

Through mindfulness and introspection, we gain a deeper understanding of our inner selves. By observing our thoughts, emotions, and beliefs without judgment, we uncover patterns and insights that shape our lives. For example, when we become mindful of our fears and insecurities, we can trace their origins and challenge their validity. By doing so, we free ourselves from limiting beliefs, opening the door to new possibilities and opportunities for growth.

Example 3: Embracing Unity and Oneness

As we delve into the universe within, we come to realize that we are not isolated individuals, but interconnected beings sharing a collective existence. Our actions and intentions reverberate through the web of life, affecting the world around us. For instance, acts of kindness and compassion not only bring joy to others but also contribute to the elevation of the collective consciousness. By embracing this interconnectedness, we cultivate empathy and a sense of responsibility for the well-being of all living beings.

Example 4: The Cosmic Dance of Synchronicity

As we become more attuned to the universe within, we notice the subtle synchronicities that guide our paths. These meaningful coincidences seem to align with our intentions and point us in the right direction. For instance, meeting someone who shares our vision or stumbling upon an opportunity at the perfect moment are all examples of the cosmic dance of synchronicity. By embracing these signs, we gain confidence in our connection with the universe and trust in the unfolding of our journey.

Example 5: Empowerment through Cosmic Awareness

The unveiling of the universe within empowers us to create positive change in our lives and the world. By aligning with the universal flow and accessing cosmic energy, we can manifest our dreams and desires. For example, a person seeking to change careers might find themselves drawn to specific opportunities or encounters that lead them towards their true calling. This cosmic awareness enables us to live authentically and with purpose, guided by the inner knowing that we are co-creators of our reality.

In this chapter of unveiling the universe within, we come to recognize that our inner selves hold the keys to profound wisdom, interconnectedness, and empowerment. By exploring and embracing the vastness of our inner universe, we unlock the potential to lead a life filled with purpose, harmony, and a deep sense of oneness with the cosmos.

- *Discovering the interconnectedness between the universe and your inner self*

Once upon a time, in a quaint little village nestled amidst a breathtaking landscape, lived a young woman named Maya. Maya was curious and adventurous, always seeking to unravel the mysteries of life. One day, she set out on a solitary journey to the nearby forest, drawn by an inexplicable calling.

As Maya wandered deeper into the woods, she felt a profound sense of peace and harmony enveloping her. She marveled at the towering trees that reached towards the heavens and the gentle rustle of leaves in the breeze. It was as if the forest itself was whispering ancient wisdom to her soul.

Lost in her thoughts, Maya came across a wise old sage sitting under the shade of a majestic oak tree. The sage smiled warmly at her and invited her to sit beside him. Intrigued by the sage's presence, Maya couldn't resist engaging in conversation.

The sage spoke of the interconnectedness between all living beings and the universe, explaining how the same cosmic energy that animated the stars and planets also resided within every living creature, including Maya herself. He likened the universe to a vast web, where every action and intention had a ripple effect on the entire fabric of existence.

As Maya listened intently, her heart felt as if it were expanding, and a deep sense of belonging washed over her. She realized that she was not separate from the grand cosmos but intricately woven into its tapestry.

The sage encouraged Maya to close her eyes and connect with her inner self, to listen to the whispers of her soul and embrace the interconnectedness she felt. As she did so, she experienced a profound awakening. She felt the pulsating energy of the universe flowing through her, and a sense of oneness with all living beings.

In that moment of connection, Maya understood that her dreams and intentions were not isolated wishes but an integral part of the cosmic dance. She realized that the universe responded to the energy she emanated, and her thoughts shaped her reality.

With newfound awareness, Maya returned to her village, carrying the wisdom of interconnectedness in her heart. She lived each day with intention, mindful of her actions, and embracing compassion for all beings. Maya's presence touched the lives of those around her, inspiring them to embark on their own journeys of self-discovery and inner connection.

As the years passed, Maya's understanding of the interconnectedness between the universe and her inner self deepened. She became a beacon of light, guiding others towards their true essence and the wonders of the universe within.

And so, Maya's journey of discovering the interconnectedness between the universe and her inner self became a timeless tale of awakening and transformation, reminding us all that we are not mere observers in the grand cosmos, but active participants in the cosmic symphony of life.

- *Awakening to the cosmic energy that resides within you*

In a bustling city, amidst the hustle and bustle of modern life, there lived a young man named Alex. Alex was successful in his career, but he felt a lingering sense of emptiness within. He yearned for something more meaningful, a deeper connection with himself and the world around him.

One day, by a stroke of fate, Alex stumbled upon a meditation workshop led by a wise spiritual teacher named Guruji. Intrigued, he decided to attend, hoping to find some solace for the restlessness in his heart.

During the workshop, Guruji guided the participants through a series of meditative practices to quiet the mind and open the heart. As Alex closed his eyes and followed the instructions, he felt a profound shift within himself. It was as if he had tapped into a wellspring of energy and wisdom he had never known existed.

As the meditation continued, Alex began to experience a heightened awareness of the world around him. He felt a sense of unity with nature, the hum of the city, and the people passing by. It was as if he could feel the interconnectedness between all living beings and the universe itself.

In that transformative moment, Alex felt the cosmic energy that resided within him. He understood that he was not separate from the universe but a part of it, connected by the same divine energy that animated the stars and galaxies.

From that day forward, Alex delved deeper into his spiritual journey, exploring various practices to awaken and harness the cosmic energy within. Through daily meditation and mindfulness, he found a sense of peace and purpose that had eluded him before.

The awakened cosmic energy within Alex propelled him to make positive changes in his life. He became more compassionate and understanding towards others, recognizing the interconnectedness of their journeys with his own. He embraced a healthier lifestyle, nurturing his body and mind with love and care.

As Alex continued to cultivate this connection with the universe within, he found the courage to pursue his true passions and dreams. He embarked on a mission to spread love and positivity in the world, inspiring others to awaken to their inner potential.

In time, Alex's newfound cosmic awareness and inner energy touched the lives of many. He became a beacon of light, guiding others towards their own awakening and reminding them that the source of power and wisdom they sought was already within them.

And so, Alex's journey of awakening to the cosmic energy within became a testament to the profound transformation that occurs when one embraces the interconnectedness between their inner self and the vast universe. It serves as a reminder to us all that the universe's boundless energy resides within each of us, waiting to be discovered, harnessed, and shared with the world.

Chapter 3
Cracking the Code to Self-Discovery

In this enlightening chapter, we embark on a transformative journey of self-exploration and introspection, cracking the code to unlock the mysteries of our true essence. Self-discovery is a sacred pilgrimage that leads us to uncover the hidden facets of our being, revealing the keys to our authentic self.

Example 1: Nurturing Self-Awareness

The first step in cracking the code to self-discovery is nurturing self-awareness. Through introspection and mindfulness, we begin to observe our thoughts, emotions, and actions without judgment. This heightened awareness allows us to identify patterns, limiting beliefs, and areas of growth. For instance, a person might recognize patterns of self-doubt holding them back in their personal or professional life. With self-awareness, they gain the power to challenge these patterns and replace them with empowering beliefs, leading to profound personal growth.

Example 2: Uncovering Your True Essence

As we delve deeper into the journey of self-discovery, we peel away the layers of conditioning and societal expectations to uncover our true essence. This process involves connecting with our passions, values, and innate talents. For example, an individual might discover a deep passion for art that they had suppressed due to external pressures. Embracing this essence allows them to express their creativity authentically and find fulfillment in their creative pursuits.

Example 3: The Power of Introspection and Reflection

Self-discovery is not just a one-time event but an ongoing process that requires regular introspection and reflection. By setting aside time for contemplation, we gain insights into our personal growth and the experiences that shape us. For instance, reflecting on past challenges and how we overcame them can illuminate our strengths and resilience. This understanding equips us with valuable lessons to navigate future obstacles with grace and wisdom.

Example 4: Embracing Vulnerability and Shadows

Cracking the code to self-discovery also involves embracing vulnerability and confronting our shadows. It requires the courage to acknowledge our fears, insecurities, and past traumas. By facing these aspects of ourselves, we heal and integrate them into our wholeness. For example, a person might confront a fear of failure that has held them back from taking risks. By embracing this vulnerability, they find the strength to pursue their dreams, knowing that failure is a stepping stone to growth.

Example 5: Cultivating Self-Compassion

Throughout the journey of self-discovery, it is vital to cultivate self-compassion. We must treat ourselves with the same kindness and understanding we extend to others. Instead of being self-critical, we learn to embrace our imperfections and mistakes as part of our human experience. This self-compassion allows us to embrace our authentic selves fully, free from the burden of self-judgment.

In cracking the code to self-discovery, we unlock the doors to profound transformation and inner growth. By nurturing self-awareness, uncovering our true essence, and embracing vulnerability with compassion, we become more in tune with our authentic selves. This heightened self-awareness leads us on a path of empowerment, self-acceptance, and a deeper connection with our true essence. As we continue to crack the code of self-discovery, we gain the keys to unlocking our unlimited potential and live a life of authenticity and fulfillment.

- *Nurturing self-awareness and uncovering your true essence*

Nurturing self-awareness and uncovering your true essence is a pivotal aspect of the journey of self-discovery. It involves delving into the depths of our being, peeling back the layers of conditioning, and gaining profound insights into our thoughts, emotions, and actions.

To nurture self-awareness, we must cultivate a practice of mindfulness and introspection. By taking moments of stillness and reflection, we become attuned to our inner world, observing our thoughts without judgment and becoming aware of our emotional responses. This heightened self-awareness allows us to recognize patterns and triggers, enabling us to respond to situations with greater clarity and emotional intelligence.

As we nurture self-awareness, we begin to uncover our true essence—the core of who we are beneath societal expectations and external influences. This essence is the embodiment of our authentic self, with unique passions, values, and talents that make us who we are.

Uncovering our true essence involves connecting with our deepest desires and passions. It is about listening to the yearnings of our heart and acknowledging what truly brings us joy and fulfillment. For instance, a person may discover a deep love for nature and the environment, which ignites a sense of purpose to advocate for sustainability and conservation.

In this journey of self-discovery, we may also encounter aspects of ourselves that have been suppressed or hidden. We may have internalized limiting beliefs or negative self-perceptions that obstruct our true essence from shining through. By uncovering these barriers, we can work towards releasing them and embracing the authentic expression of who we are.

Through the process of nurturing self-awareness and uncovering our true essence, we gain a sense of inner alignment and harmony. We become more confident in our choices, knowing that they align with our core values and aspirations. This self-awareness empowers us to make decisions that resonate with our authentic self, leading to a more fulfilling and purposeful life.

As we continue to nurture self-awareness and uncover our true essence, we develop a deeper connection with ourselves and a profound appreciation for our unique qualities. This journey of self-discovery is ongoing, and as we explore the depths of our being, we unlock the potential for personal growth, self-acceptance, and a meaningful connection with the world around us. Ultimately, it is through this process that we find the keys to unlocking the fullness of our true selves and living a life that reflects our genuine essence.

- *Harnessing the power of introspection and reflection*

Harnessing the power of introspection and reflection is a transformative practice that empowers us to gain deep insights into ourselves and our life experiences. It is a process of self-examination that allows us to understand the patterns, beliefs, and behaviors that shape our lives.

Through introspection, we turn our attention inward, exploring our thoughts, emotions, and motivations. It is a quiet and contemplative process, where we ask ourselves meaningful questions and seek honest answers. By engaging in introspection, we uncover the layers of our inner world, discovering the roots of our desires, fears, and aspirations.

Reflection, on the other hand, is the act of looking back on our experiences and learning from them. It is an opportunity to gain wisdom from both our successes and our challenges. Through reflection, we recognize the lessons life has taught us and how they have contributed to our growth and development.

When we harness the power of introspection and reflection, several transformative outcomes emerge:

Self-awareness: Introspection and reflection foster self-awareness, allowing us to better understand our strengths, weaknesses, and areas for improvement. This self-awareness empowers us to make conscious choices aligned with our values and goals.

Emotional intelligence: By delving into our emotions through introspection, we enhance our emotional intelligence. We become more in tune with our feelings, enabling us to navigate them with greater ease and empathy towards ourselves and others.

Personal growth: Introspection and reflection act as catalysts for personal growth and development. By recognizing patterns and areas that need attention, we can embark on a journey of continuous self-improvement.

Decision-making: When we engage in introspection and reflection, we gain clarity and insight into our life choices. This clarity empowers us to make decisions that align with our authentic selves and long-term aspirations.

Gratitude and resilience: Reflection allows us to appreciate our accomplishments and acknowledge our resilience in overcoming challenges. Gratitude for our journey nurtures a positive outlook and fosters resilience in the face of adversity.

Empathy and understanding: Introspection not only deepens our understanding of ourselves but also enhances our empathy and understanding towards others. As we recognize and accept our imperfections, we extend the same compassion to those around us.

Harnessing the power of introspection and reflection is an ongoing practice that leads to greater self-awareness, personal growth, and a more meaningful and intentional life. By carving out time for self-exploration and learning from our experiences, we unlock the keys to living with authenticity, purpose, and a deeper sense of fulfillment.

Chapter 4
Cultivating Inner Strength and Resilience

In this empowering chapter, we delve into the process of cultivating inner strength and resilience, recognizing that they are essential qualities that enable us to navigate life's challenges with grace and fortitude. It is a transformative journey that empowers us to tap into the wellspring of strength within, fostering a deep sense of self-belief and unwavering determination.

Example 1: Tapping into the Inner Reservoir of Strength

Cultivating inner strength begins by acknowledging that we possess an inner reservoir of resilience and power. Like a well, this strength is always available to draw upon, even during the most trying times. For instance, when faced with a daunting life transition, such as a career change or loss, tapping into this inner strength allows us to stay grounded and steadfast in our pursuit of new opportunities.

Example 2: Building Resilience in the Face of Adversity

Resilience is a remarkable quality that allows us to bounce back from setbacks and learn from adversity. Cultivating resilience involves reframing challenges as opportunities for growth and learning. For instance, when faced with failure, a resilient individual embraces it as a stepping stone towards future success, using the experience to acquire valuable lessons and insights.

Example 3: Embracing Self-Compassion and Self-Care

Cultivating inner strength and resilience also entails embracing self-compassion and practicing self-care. Acknowledging that we are human and not immune to vulnerabilities allows us to treat ourselves with kindness and understanding. For instance, during periods of stress or overwhelming demands, practicing self-care through relaxation techniques or seeking support from loved ones nurtures our resilience and restores balance to our lives.

Example 4: The Power of Positive Mindset

A positive mindset plays a pivotal role in cultivating inner strength and resilience. By adopting a growth-oriented perspective, we view challenges as opportunities for growth and transformation. For instance, a person facing a career setback may choose to view it as a chance to explore new career paths and unearth untapped potential.

Example 5: Drawing Inspiration from Role Models

Cultivating inner strength and resilience can be further supported by drawing inspiration from role models who have demonstrated unwavering strength in the face of adversity. Learning from the experiences of others and witnessing their resilience encourages us to cultivate similar qualities within ourselves.

Through the journey of cultivating inner strength and resilience, we develop an unshakable foundation that enables us to stand strong amidst life's trials and tribulations. This inner fortitude empowers us to embrace challenges with courage, trusting in our ability to overcome obstacles and emerge stronger on the other side. As we tap into our inner strength and nurture resilience, we embark on a transformative path that allows us to face life's uncertainties with confidence, grace, and an unwavering belief in our capacity to thrive.

- *Tapping into your inner reservoir of strength*

Tapping into your inner reservoir of strength is a transformative process that empowers you to harness the boundless wellspring of power and resilience that resides within. It involves recognizing that you possess the capacity to face life's challenges with unwavering determination and courage.

The journey of tapping into your inner reservoir of strength begins with self-awareness and self-belief. By acknowledging your inherent worth and potential, you lay the foundation for accessing the well of strength within you. It is about recognizing that you are not defined by your past or present circumstances, but by the limitless potential that lies within.

As you delve deeper into this journey, you cultivate a positive mindset and embrace a growth-oriented perspective. Instead of viewing obstacles as insurmountable barriers, you see them as opportunities for learning and growth. With this mindset, you are better equipped to draw valuable lessons from adversity and use them as stepping stones towards personal development.

Tapping into your inner reservoir of strength also involves embracing self-compassion and practicing self-care. Acknowledging that you are human and that it is natural to face challenges allows you to treat yourself with kindness and understanding. By prioritizing self-care, you replenish your emotional, mental, and physical energy, nurturing your resilience and fortitude.

This transformative journey is about connecting with your authentic self and listening to the whispers of your soul. It is a process of trusting your intuition and following your heart's desires. By aligning with your true essence, you gain a profound sense of purpose and direction, which empowers you to overcome obstacles with clarity and determination.

Throughout this journey, drawing inspiration from role models and individuals who have demonstrated inner strength can be immensely valuable. Learning from their experiences and witnessing their resilience serves as a guiding light, encouraging you to tap into your own inner reservoir of strength.

As you tap into your inner reservoir of strength, you become a source of inspiration and empowerment for yourself and others. You navigate life's challenges with unwavering confidence and embrace the journey with a profound sense of self-assurance. The inner strength you cultivate becomes a guiding force, allowing you to navigate the currents of life with grace, courage, and an unyielding belief in your ability to thrive.

- *Building resilience to overcome challenges and adversity*

Building resilience is a transformative process that empowers individuals to overcome challenges and adversity with strength, adaptability, and perseverance. It is the capacity to bounce back from setbacks, learn from difficult experiences, and emerge stronger and more resourceful.

The journey of building resilience begins with embracing the idea that challenges are a natural part of life. By accepting that adversity is inevitable, individuals can develop a mindset that views challenges as opportunities for growth and learning. This positive perspective lays the groundwork for resilience.

In the face of challenges, individuals build resilience by cultivating emotional intelligence. They acknowledge and process their feelings, allowing themselves to experience a full range of emotions without judgment. Embracing vulnerability and seeking support from loved ones fosters emotional resilience and strengthens the capacity to cope with stress.

Another key aspect of building resilience is developing problem-solving skills. Resilient individuals approach challenges with a solution-oriented mindset, exploring different strategies to overcome obstacles. They are willing to adapt and adjust their approach when needed, demonstrating flexibility and resourcefulness in finding solutions.

Resilience is also nurtured through a sense of purpose and meaning. By connecting with personal values and goals, individuals can anchor themselves during difficult times, finding motivation to persevere and stay focused on their aspirations.

The practice of self-compassion is vital in building resilience. Treating oneself with kindness and understanding during challenging moments fosters self-esteem and a sense of inner strength. Individuals who are compassionate towards themselves are better equipped to weather difficulties and emerge with greater resilience.

Additionally, embracing a growth mindset plays a pivotal role in building resilience. This mindset recognizes that failures and setbacks are opportunities for learning and growth. Resilient individuals view challenges as stepping stones, rather than roadblocks, on their journey to success.

Building resilience is an ongoing journey, and setbacks are an integral part of the process. Resilient individuals understand that setbacks do not define them but serve as valuable lessons to be learned and integrated into their growth.

Ultimately, the journey of building resilience equips individuals with the tools and inner fortitude to navigate life's challenges with grace and determination. As they face adversity, they draw upon their resilience to stand strong, adapt, and continue moving forward. Through this transformative process, they emerge as individuals who can thrive in the face of uncertainty and use challenges as stepping stones towards personal growth and fulfillment.

Chapter 5
Aligning with Cosmic Energy

In this enlightening chapter, we explore the profound practice of aligning with cosmic energy—an ancient wisdom that empowers us to harmonize with the universal flow and manifest our deepest desires and intentions. Aligning with cosmic energy is a transformative journey of connecting with the interconnected web of existence and recognizing our inherent oneness with the cosmos.

Example 1: Embracing the Universal Flow

Aligning with cosmic energy begins with embracing the universal flow, recognizing that everything in the universe is interconnected and governed by a divine rhythm. By attuning ourselves to this flow, we learn to let go of resistance and surrender to the natural unfolding of life. For instance, when faced with unexpected changes, aligning with cosmic energy allows us to find peace and trust that there is a higher purpose guiding us.

Example 2: Practicing Mindfulness and Presence

Mindfulness and presence are powerful tools in aligning with cosmic energy. By living in the present moment, we detach ourselves from the past and future, allowing us to fully experience the beauty and abundance of the present. Mindfulness helps us tap into the energy of the now, enabling us to make conscious choices that align with our authentic selves.

Example 3: Gratitude and Appreciation

Practicing gratitude and appreciation is an essential aspect of aligning with cosmic energy. By expressing gratitude for the blessings and abundance in our lives, we open ourselves to receiving more. This practice of gratitude raises our vibration, aligning us with positive energy and attracting more of what we desire.

Example 4: Setting Clear Intentions

Aligning with cosmic energy involves setting clear intentions for our lives. By defining our goals and desires, we send a powerful message to the universe about what we want to manifest. When our intentions are aligned with our values and higher purpose, we become co-creators of our reality, working in harmony with cosmic energy to manifest our dreams.

Example 5: Connecting with Nature and the Cosmos

Spending time in nature and observing the celestial wonders of the cosmos is a powerful way to align with cosmic energy. Nature is a reflection of the universal flow, and by immersing ourselves in its beauty, we strengthen our connection with the cosmic forces at play. Gazing at the stars, we are reminded of our place in the vastness of the universe, fostering a sense of awe and interconnectedness.

Through the journey of aligning with cosmic energy, we become attuned to the abundant and limitless possibilities that the universe offers. By embracing the universal flow, practicing mindfulness, expressing gratitude, setting clear intentions, and connecting with nature and the cosmos, we tap into our innate power as co-creators of our reality. This transformative alignment empowers us to live with purpose, passion, and a profound sense of harmony with the grand cosmic dance of existence.

- *Harmonizing your energy with the universal flow*

Harmonizing your energy with the universal flow is a profound practice that allows you to align your inner vibrations with the natural rhythms of the cosmos. It involves tuning into the interconnectedness of all life and embracing the inherent oneness between your energy and the universal energy that permeates everything.

To harmonize your energy with the universal flow, you can explore the following steps:

Cultivate Mindfulness: Begin by cultivating mindfulness in your daily life. Pay attention to your thoughts, emotions, and actions. Notice when you feel in sync with the flow of life and when you experience resistance or discord. Mindfulness allows you to become aware of any imbalances and helps you return to a state of alignment.

Let Go of Resistance: Embrace the idea that life is ever-changing and flowing. Let go of the need to control every aspect of your existence and surrender to the natural ebb and flow of life. When you release resistance, you open yourself up to the opportunities and possibilities that the universe presents.

Practice Gratitude: Gratitude is a powerful tool for harmonizing your energy with the universal flow. Cultivate an attitude of appreciation for the blessings and experiences in your life. Expressing gratitude raises your vibration and attracts more positive energy, fostering a deeper alignment with the universe.

Connect with Nature: Spend time in nature and immerse yourself in its beauty. Nature is a reflection of the universal flow, and being in its presence helps you attune to the natural rhythms of the cosmos. Allow yourself to be present and absorb the healing energy of the natural world.

Align Your Intentions: Set clear intentions aligned with your authentic self and higher purpose. When you define your intentions, you send a powerful signal to the universe about your desires and aspirations. Be mindful of your intentions, ensuring they align with the greater good and the interconnected web of existence.

Practice Self-Care: Taking care of your physical, emotional, and spiritual well-being is essential for harmonizing your energy. Prioritize self-care activities that nourish your mind, body, and soul, such as meditation, yoga, or creative pursuits. When you are in balance and harmony within yourself, you naturally resonate with the universal flow.

Trust in the Process: Have faith in the natural order of the universe and trust that everything unfolds in divine timing. Release the need for immediate outcomes and have patience with the journey. Trusting in the process allows you to navigate life's challenges with grace and serenity.

By harmonizing your energy with the universal flow, you become a conscious participant in the cosmic dance of existence. You experience a deep sense of interconnectedness with all living beings and the vast cosmos, allowing you to live with purpose, authenticity, and a profound sense of harmony with the greater rhythms of life. This alignment empowers you to navigate life's journey with grace and wisdom, manifesting your dreams and aspirations with a deep understanding of your place in the grand tapestry of the universe.

- *Harnessing the power of alignment for manifestation*

Harnessing the power of alignment for manifestation is a transformative practice that empowers you to co-create your reality in harmony with the universal flow. It involves aligning your thoughts, emotions, beliefs, and actions with your intentions and desires, allowing you to manifest your dreams and aspirations with greater ease and effectiveness.

To harness the power of alignment for manifestation, consider the following steps:

Clarity of Intentions: Begin by gaining clarity about your intentions and desires. Clearly define what you want to manifest in your life, whether it's related to personal growth, career, relationships, or any other area. The more precise and specific you are about your intentions, the easier it becomes to align your energy towards their manifestation.

Positive Affirmations: Use positive affirmations to reinforce your intentions and beliefs. Affirmations are powerful statements that help reprogram your subconscious mind, aligning it with your desires. Repeat affirmations regularly, focusing on the positive outcomes you want to manifest.

Visualization: Practice visualization to bring your intentions to life. Close your eyes and vividly imagine yourself already living your desired reality. Engage all your senses to feel the emotions, sights, sounds, and sensations associated with achieving your goals. Visualization enhances your alignment with the energy of manifestation.

Gratitude and Trust: Cultivate gratitude for what you have and trust in the manifestation process. Express gratitude for the things you already have and the progress you've made towards your goals. Trust that the universe is working in your favor and that your intentions will manifest at the perfect time.

Release Resistance: Identify and release any limiting beliefs or resistance that may hinder your alignment with manifestation. Address any doubts or fears that arise and replace them with positive, empowering beliefs. Embrace a mindset of abundance and possibility.

Act with Intention: Take inspired action towards your goals. Align your actions with your intentions, making conscious choices that support your manifestation process. Take steps that move you closer to your desired outcomes, and trust that each action is a powerful contribution to the manifestation of your dreams.

Remain open and Receptive: Stay open and receptive to the signs and opportunities that present themselves along the way. The universe may provide unexpected pathways to manifest your intentions, and being open allows you to recognize and seize these opportunities.

Patience and Surrender: Practice patience and surrender in the manifestation process. Avoid forcing outcomes or becoming attached to specific timelines. Trust in divine timing and know that the universe will align all elements for your highest good.

By harnessing the power of alignment for manifestation, you become a conscious co-creator of your reality. As you align your thoughts, beliefs, emotions, and actions with your intentions, you create a powerful synergy with the universal flow, allowing your dreams and aspirations to manifest with greater ease and divine grace. This transformative alignment empowers you to live a life of purpose, fulfillment, and abundance, as you embrace the magic of co-creating with the universe.

Chapter 6
Activating Your Inner Potential

In this empowering chapter, we embark on a transformative journey of self-discovery and self-empowerment, unlocking the gates to our inner potential. Activating our inner potential is about unleashing our unique gifts, talents, and abilities to live a purposeful and fulfilling life.

Example 1: Unleashing Your Unique Gifts and Talents

Activating your inner potential involves recognizing and embracing your unique gifts and talents. Take time to explore your passions and interests, and identify the skills that come naturally to you. When you tap into your innate abilities, you unleash a wellspring of creativity and inspiration that can lead to extraordinary achievements.

Example 2: Empowering Yourself to Pursue Your Dreams

Activating your inner potential requires courage and determination to pursue your dreams. It is about believing in yourself and your capabilities, even when faced with challenges and self-doubt. By stepping out of your comfort zone and taking action towards your aspirations, you create opportunities for personal growth and transformation.

Example 3: Embracing Lifelong Learning and Growth

Activating your inner potential is an ongoing process of learning and growth. Embrace a mindset of curiosity and continuous improvement. Seek out new knowledge, acquire new skills, and be open to feedback and constructive criticism. Embracing lifelong learning expands your horizons and enables you to adapt to changing circumstances.

Example 4: Setting Meaningful Goals

To activate your inner potential, set meaningful and achievable goals aligned with your values and vision. Break down your goals into smaller, manageable steps, and celebrate each milestone you achieve. Setting clear intentions propels you forward and keeps you focused on your path of personal development and success.

Example 5: Overcoming Limiting Beliefs

Activating your inner potential involves identifying and overcoming limiting beliefs that may hold you back. Challenge negative thought patterns and replace them with empowering beliefs that affirm your worth and capabilities. As you release self-imposed limitations, you free yourself to explore new possibilities and reach greater heights.

Example 6: Embodying Self-Confidence

Embodying self-confidence is a key aspect of activating your inner potential. Believe in yourself and your capacity to achieve your goals. Cultivate self-assurance and approach challenges with a positive mindset. With self-confidence, you radiate a magnetic energy that attracts opportunities and empowers you to overcome obstacles.

Through the journey of activating your inner potential, you unleash the power to create a life that reflects your true essence. By embracing your unique gifts, empowering yourself to pursue your dreams, and nurturing a growth-oriented mindset, you tap into the limitless well of possibilities within. As you set meaningful goals, overcome limiting beliefs, and embody self-confidence, you become the master of your destiny, unlocking your true potential and living a purposeful, meaningful, and fulfilled life.

- *Unleashing your unique gifts and talents*

Unleashing your unique gifts and talents is a transformative journey of self-discovery and self-expression, allowing you to tap into your innate abilities and share them with the world. Embracing and honing your gifts enables you to live a life of purpose and fulfillment, leaving a positive impact on those around you.

Self-Exploration: Unleashing your unique gifts and talents begins with self-exploration. Take the time to reflect on your passions, interests, and what brings you joy. Identify the activities that come naturally to you and energize you. This process of self-discovery helps you uncover your hidden talents and areas of strength.

Embrace Your Authenticity: Embrace your authenticity and honor what makes you unique. Celebrate your individuality and recognize that your gifts are special and valuable. Embracing your authentic self allows you to express your talents with confidence and genuine passion.

Cultivate Self-Belief: Cultivate self-belief and have faith in your abilities. Recognize that you have something valuable to offer and that your gifts have the power to make a difference. Trust in your potential and know that you are worthy of success and recognition.

Practice and Develop: Unleashing your gifts and talents requires practice and development. Invest time in honing your skills, refining your craft, and continuously improving. Embrace a growth mindset and be open to learning from experiences and challenges.

Share Your Gifts: Share your gifts and talents with the world. Whether it's through creative expression, helping others, or contributing to a cause you believe in, allow your unique abilities to shine. Sharing your gifts not only brings joy and fulfillment to your life but also has a positive impact on others.

Embrace Challenges: Embrace challenges and view them as opportunities for growth. Stepping outside your comfort zone allows you to discover new aspects of your abilities and unlock hidden potentials. Embrace setbacks as valuable learning experiences that propel you forward on your journey of unleashing your gifts.

Surround Yourself with Supportive People: Surround yourself with supportive and encouraging individuals who believe in your potential. Seek mentors, friends, or a community that nurtures your talents and offers constructive feedback. Positive support can fuel your confidence and help you thrive.

Remain Humble: As you unleash your unique gifts and talents, remain humble and open to learning from others. Recognize that everyone has something to offer, and there is always room for growth and improvement. Humility allows you to stay open-minded and continue evolving as a person.

By unleashing your unique gifts and talents, you become the best version of yourself, contributing your authentic self to the world. Embrace your uniqueness, cultivate self-belief, and share your gifts with confidence and humility. As you do so, you create a ripple effect of inspiration and empowerment, touching the lives of others and leaving a lasting legacy of positivity and authenticity.

Chapter 7
The Cosmic Connection: Intuition and Guidance

In this enlightening chapter, we explore the profound connection between intuition and cosmic guidance—a transformative partnership that empowers us to tap into the universal intelligence and receive guidance from the vast cosmic realms.

Embracing Intuitive Wisdom: Embracing intuitive wisdom involves acknowledging the innate wisdom that resides within us. Intuition is our inner guidance system—a deep knowing that transcends logic and reasoning. By tuning into our intuition, we access valuable insights and make decisions aligned with our authentic selves.

Cultivating Intuitive Awareness: Cultivating intuitive awareness is a practice of mindfulness and presence. By quieting the noise of the external world and turning inward, we attune ourselves to the subtle whispers of our intuition. Through meditation, contemplation, or spending time in nature, we deepen our connection with our intuitive self.

Trusting the Universal Flow: Trusting the universal flow is about surrendering to the divine intelligence that orchestrates the cosmos. It involves having faith that the universe conspires in our favor and supports our journey. Trusting the universal flow allows us to let go of control and embrace the guidance that comes our way.

Recognizing Synchronicities: Synchronicities are meaningful coincidences that are signs from the universe. By being open and observant, we recognize synchronicities as subtle messages guiding us towards our path. When we pay attention to these signs, we align ourselves with the cosmic flow and receive the guidance we need.

Seeking Guidance from Higher Realms: Seeking guidance from higher realms involves connecting with spiritual guides, angels, or higher beings. Through meditation, prayer, or intention-setting, we invite their guidance into our lives. This connection allows us to receive insights and support from realms beyond the physical.

Listening to the Wisdom of the Heart: The heart is a powerful center of intuitive wisdom. By listening to the wisdom of the heart, we make decisions that resonate with our deepest desires and values. When we align with the heart's guidance, we lead a life that is authentic and fulfilling.

Honoring Inner Knowing: Honoring our inner knowing is about having the courage to follow our intuition, even when it goes against conventional wisdom. By trusting our gut feelings and inner guidance, we embrace the unique path that the universe has in store for us.

Integration of Intuition and Logic: Integrating intuition and logic allows us to make balanced decisions. While intuition provides valuable insights, logic and critical thinking help us assess practical aspects. By combining both, we make grounded choices in alignment with our higher purpose.

Through the cosmic connection of intuition and guidance, we gain access to a vast reservoir of wisdom and support. By embracing our intuitive nature, trusting the universal flow, and seeking guidance from higher realms, we receive profound insights that illuminate our path. This transformative connection empowers us to navigate life with clarity, authenticity, and a deep sense of alignment with the greater cosmic plan.

- *Deepening your connection to the universal intelligence*

Deepening your connection to the universal intelligence is a profound and transformative journey that allows you to tap into the boundless wisdom and guidance of the cosmos. It involves opening your heart and mind to the vastness of the universe, recognizing your inherent connection to all that is, and attuning yourself to the higher realms of knowledge.

Practice Mindfulness and Presence: Mindfulness and presence are essential in deepening your connection to universal intelligence. By living in the present moment and quieting the constant chatter of the mind, you create space to tune into the subtle messages and insights that the universe offers.

Embrace Oneness: Embrace the concept of oneness, recognizing that you are an integral part of the interconnected web of existence. When you understand that everything is interconnected, you open yourself to receive guidance from the collective consciousness of the universe.

Meditate and Contemplate: Meditation and contemplation are powerful practices to deepen your connection to universal intelligence. Through meditation, you access deeper states of consciousness, allowing you to receive intuitive guidance and spiritual insights. Contemplation on profound questions and universal truths also opens your mind to higher wisdom.

Connect with Nature: Spending time in nature helps you connect with the rhythms and energies of the natural world, which are reflections of the universal intelligence. Nature serves as a mirror to our inner landscape, fostering a sense of harmony and unity with the cosmos.

Seek Knowledge and Wisdom: Seek knowledge and wisdom from various sources, including ancient teachings, spiritual texts, and wise teachers. Engaging in learning broadens your understanding of universal principles and empowers you to apply them in your life.

Trust Your Intuition: Trusting your intuition is key to deepening your connection to the universal intelligence. The more you trust and act upon your intuitive insights, the stronger your connection becomes. Intuition is a direct channel to the higher realms of wisdom.

Practice Gratitude: Cultivate an attitude of gratitude for the abundance of wisdom and guidance that the universe provides. Expressing gratitude opens your heart and aligns your energy with the flow of universal intelligence.

Surrender and Let Go: Surrendering and letting go of the need to control allows you to be receptive to the wisdom of the universe. When you release attachments and surrender to the greater plan, you align yourself with the cosmic flow and receive divine guidance.

Through the journey of deepening your connection to universal intelligence, you expand your consciousness, gain profound insights, and experience a deep sense of unity with all of creation. As you attune yourself to the higher realms of knowledge, you walk a path of wisdom, authenticity, and inner peace, guided by the loving intelligence of the cosmos. This transformative connection empowers you to live with purpose, clarity, and a profound sense of alignment with the greater mysteries of existence.

- *Trusting your intuition and accessing divine guidance*

Trusting your intuition and accessing divine guidance is a transformative process that empowers you to tap into the profound wisdom of the universe and align with your true path. It involves developing a deep sense of trust in your inner knowing and opening yourself to receive guidance from the higher realms of existence.

Cultivate Self-Awareness: Cultivating self-awareness is essential in trusting your intuition. Pay attention to your feelings, sensations, and gut instincts. Listen to the quiet voice within that offers insights and guidance. The more you tune into your inner wisdom, the stronger your intuitive abilities become.

Recognize the Difference: Learn to discern between the voice of intuition and the chatter of the mind. Intuition often comes as a gentle, peaceful knowing, while the mind can be filled with doubt and fear. Trust in the clarity and certainty of your intuitive guidance.

Follow Inspired Action: When you receive intuitive guidance, be willing to take inspired action. Trust that the universe is guiding you in the right direction. Even if the path may seem uncertain, have faith in the wisdom of the guidance received.

Practice Meditation and Stillness: Regular meditation and moments of stillness help you connect with divine guidance. In silence, you can hear the whispers of the universe, and through meditation, you open channels to receive profound insights and messages.

Surrender and Let Go: Surrender to the divine flow and let go of the need to control every aspect of your life. Trust that there is a higher intelligence guiding you and that everything is unfolding as it should. Embrace the concept of divine timing and divine order.

Connect with Spirituality: Embrace a spiritual practice that resonates with you. This could include prayer, ritual, or connecting with your higher self. Strengthening your spiritual connection enhances your ability to access divine guidance.

Seek Signs and Synchronicities: Pay attention to signs and synchronicities that appear in your life. These are often messages from the universe, guiding you on your path. Trust in the timing and significance of these signs.

Journal and Reflect: Keep a journal of your intuitive experiences and insights. Writing down your thoughts and reflections helps you deepen your connection to divine guidance and provides a record of your spiritual journey.

Trusting your intuition and accessing divine guidance is a profound partnership that brings clarity, purpose, and serenity to your life. As you cultivate trust in your inner knowing and open yourself to the wisdom of the universe, you walk a path of alignment and authenticity. Embracing this transformative connection empowers you to make decisions with confidence, navigate challenges with grace, and embrace the unfolding of your life's journey with a profound sense of divine guidance and support.

Chapter 8
The Power of Intention and Visualization

In this empowering chapter, we delve into the profound impact of intention and visualization in shaping our reality and manifesting our desires. The power of intention and visualization is a transformative force that allows us to consciously create our lives and align with the cosmic flow of manifestation.

Setting Clear Intentions: Setting clear intentions is the foundation of harnessing this power. Define your goals and desires with precision, clarity, and positivity. Intention-setting focuses your energy and sends a powerful message to the universe about what you wish to attract into your life.

Affirming Positive Beliefs: Affirmations play a pivotal role in supporting your intentions. Craft positive and empowering affirmations that reinforce your beliefs in your capabilities and the abundance of the universe.

Repetition of these affirmations helps rewire your subconscious mind, aligning it with your intentions.

Visualization as Creative Imagination: Visualization is the art of creative imagination. Envision yourself already living your intentions as if they have already manifested. Engage all your senses to feel the emotions, sights, sounds, and sensations associated with your desired reality. Visualization strengthens your alignment with the energy of manifestation.

Creating Vision Boards: Vision boards are powerful tools that bring your intentions to life. Create a visual representation of your goals and aspirations, using images, words, and symbols that resonate with you. Placing your vision board where you can see it daily reinforces your intentions and keeps you focused on your path.

Engaging Emotional Energy: Infuse your intentions and visualizations with powerful emotions. Emotions are energy in motion and serve as magnets for manifestation. Feel genuine joy, gratitude, and excitement as you visualize your desires, knowing that the universe responds to the energy you emit.

Letting Go and Surrendering: Once you have set your intentions and visualized your desired reality, release the need to control the how and when of manifestation. Surrender your desires to the universal intelligence, trusting that everything unfolds in divine timing and in the best way possible.

Taking Inspired Action: While intention and visualization are potent forces, they are most effective when combined with inspired action. Be open to opportunities and take steps towards your goals. Align your actions with your intentions, knowing that every action is a co-creative effort with the universe.

Gratitude for Manifestation: Practice gratitude for the manifestation of your intentions, even before they fully materialize. Cultivate an attitude of appreciation for the progress you make and the signs of alignment that appear along the way. Gratitude magnifies the energy of manifestation.

Through the power of intention and visualization, you become a conscious co-creator of your reality. As you set clear intentions, affirm positive beliefs, and engage in creative visualization, you tap into the limitless potential within you. Trusting in the universal flow and taking inspired action, you align with the greater cosmic plan. This transformative connection empowers you to manifest your dreams, aspirations, and desires with clarity, purpose, and a profound sense of harmony with the abundant possibilities that the universe offers.

- *Utilizing intention-setting and visualization techniques to manifest your desires*

Utilizing intention-setting and visualization techniques is a powerful approach to manifesting your desires and bringing them into reality. These practices enable you to harness the creative power of your mind and align with the universal flow of manifestation. Here's how you can use intention-setting and visualization techniques to manifest your desires:

Clarity of Intentions: Start by gaining crystal-clear clarity about what you want to manifest. Be specific and precise about your desires, whether they pertain to personal growth, career, relationships, health, or any other aspect of life. Write down your intentions, affirming them as already accomplished.

Affirmations: Create positive and empowering affirmations that support your intentions. Craft statements that reflect your desired reality and state them in the present tense. For example, if your intention is to find a fulfilling job, affirm, "I am now working in a fulfilling and rewarding job that aligns with my passion and purpose."

Visualization: Engage in regular visualization sessions where you vividly imagine yourself already living your intended reality. Picture the details, emotions, and sensations associated with achieving your goals. See yourself in the situations you desire and feel the joy and fulfillment of living that reality.

Create a Vision Board: Develop a vision board that visually represents your intentions and desires. Collect images, quotes, and symbols that resonate with your goals and arrange them on a board. Place your vision board in a prominent place where you can see it daily to reinforce your intentions.

Engage Your Senses: During visualization, engage all your senses to make the experience more vivid and compelling. Feel the textures, smell the scents, and hear the sounds associated with your desired reality. The more real and immersive you make the visualization, the stronger the impact on your subconscious mind.

Practice Daily Gratitude: Cultivate an attitude of gratitude for the manifestation of your desires, even before they have fully materialized. Express gratitude for the progress you make, the opportunities that arise, and the signs of alignment you observe. Gratitude amplifies the energy of manifestation.

Let Go and Trust: After setting your intentions and visualizing your desires, release the need to control every detail of the process. Trust in the universal intelligence and the perfect timing of the manifestation. Let go of doubts and fears, knowing that the universe is working in your favor.

Take Inspired Action: While intention-setting and visualization are potent practices, they are most effective when combined with inspired action. Be open to opportunities and take steps towards your goals. The universe responds to your co-creative efforts, so be proactive in aligning your actions with your intentions.

By utilizing intention-setting and visualization techniques, you tap into the immense power of your mind and the universal flow. Aligning your thoughts, emotions, and actions with your intentions, you become an active participant in the manifestation of your desires. Trust in the process, be persistent, and maintain a positive mindset. This transformative approach empowers you to manifest your dreams and create a life that reflects your deepest aspirations and true potential.

- *Aligning your intentions with the greater cosmic plan*

Aligning your intentions with the greater cosmic plan is a profound and transformative process that involves harmonizing your desires and goals with the higher purpose of the universe. By doing so, you tap into the universal flow and allow your intentions to be guided by the wisdom and intelligence of the cosmos. Here's how you can align your intentions with the greater cosmic plan:

Cultivate Awareness: Begin by cultivating awareness of the interconnectedness of all life. Recognize that you are an integral part of the vast web of existence and that your intentions can have far-reaching effects on the world around you.

Connect with Your Higher Self: Establish a connection with your higher self, the aspect of you that is aligned with your soul's purpose and the greater cosmic plan. Through meditation, introspection, and spiritual practices, tune into your inner guidance and wisdom.

Surrender to Divine Timing: Trust in the divine timing of events. Sometimes, the universe has a different schedule for the manifestation of your intentions than you do. Surrendering to divine timing allows you to let go of impatience and aligns you with the natural rhythms of life.

Embrace Detachment: While it's essential to set clear intentions, embrace a sense of detachment from specific outcomes. Avoid getting overly attached to how your desires should manifest. Instead, focus on the essence of what you wish to experience and remain open to various possibilities.

Listen to Intuitive Guidance: Pay attention to your intuition and inner guidance. Your intuition can offer valuable insights about whether your intentions are aligned with the greater cosmic plan. Trust your gut feelings and allow your inner wisdom to guide your decisions.

Serve the Greater Good: Align your intentions with service to the greater good. Consider how your desires can benefit not only yourself but also others and the world at large. When your intentions are rooted in compassion and love, they naturally align with the cosmic plan.

Practice Gratitude: Cultivate an attitude of gratitude for the opportunities, lessons, and synchronicities that arise as you align with the cosmic plan. Expressing gratitude acknowledges the support and guidance you receive from the universe.

Stay Open to Course Corrections: Be open to course corrections along the way. Sometimes, the universe may guide you to take a different path that better aligns with your soul's growth and the cosmic plan. Be flexible and receptive to these shifts.

By aligning your intentions with the greater cosmic plan, you become a co-creator with the universe, harmonizing your desires with the higher purpose of existence.

Embrace your interconnectedness with all of creation, listen to your inner guidance, and serve the greater good. As you surrender to divine timing and remain open to the unfolding of events, you step into a flow of grace and synchronicity. This transformative alignment empowers you to live a life of purpose, fulfillment, and harmony with the grand design of the cosmos.

Chapter 9
The Journey of Self-Love and Acceptance

In this transformative chapter, we embark on a profound journey of self-discovery and inner healing—exploring the profound significance of self-love and self-acceptance in cultivating a fulfilling and authentic life.

Embracing Your Inherent Worth: The journey of self-love begins with embracing your inherent worth. Recognize that you are deserving of love, compassion, and acceptance simply because you exist. Let go of self-judgment and embrace the uniqueness that makes you who you are.

Practicing Self-Compassion: Be kind and gentle with yourself, especially during times of difficulty or perceived failure. Treat yourself with the same compassion and understanding you would offer to a dear friend. Self-compassion nurtures a deep sense of love and acceptance within.

Unearthing Self-Discovery: Engage in self-discovery to understand your true essence. Explore your passions, strengths, and values. Celebrate your strengths and acknowledge areas for growth without harsh criticism. Embrace the journey of continuous learning and self-improvement.

Healing Emotional Wounds: Healing emotional wounds is an essential aspect of self-love and acceptance. Offer yourself the space to process and release past hurts and traumas. Seek support from trusted individuals or professionals if needed. As you heal, you create room for love and acceptance to flourish.

Letting Go of Comparison: Release the need to compare yourself to others. Embrace your unique journey and avoid measuring your worth based on external achievements or societal standards. Appreciate and celebrate your individuality and the path you are walking.

Practicing Self-Care: Self-love is nurtured through self-care. Prioritize activities that nourish your physical, emotional, and spiritual well-being. Make time for hobbies, relaxation, and activities that bring you joy.

Self-care reinforces your sense of worth and love for yourself.

Affirming Positive Self-Talk: Challenge negative self-talk and replace it with empowering affirmations. Reframe self-criticism into self-encouragement and self-appreciation. Speak to yourself with kindness and positivity.

Embracing Imperfection: Embrace imperfection as a natural part of the human experience. Accept that nobody is flawless, and growth often emerges from imperfections. Embracing imperfection allows you to be authentic and real.

Cultivating Gratitude: Practice gratitude for all aspects of yourself and your life's journey. Celebrate your strengths and acknowledge the lessons learned from challenges. Gratitude fosters a deep sense of self-love and acceptance.

Forgiving Yourself: Forgive yourself for past mistakes and perceived shortcomings. Release self-blame and embrace the lessons learned from your experiences. Forgiveness liberates your heart and paves the way for greater self-love.

The journey of self-love and acceptance is an ongoing process of inner exploration, healing, and growth. As you embark on this transformative journey, you discover the beauty of embracing your authentic self. Embracing self-love and acceptance empowers you to live a life of joy, purpose, and authenticity, honoring the magnificent being that you truly are. This transformative connection fosters deep relationships with others and a profound sense of interconnectedness with the world around you.

- *Embracing self-love as the foundation of inner power*

Embracing self-love as the foundation of inner power is a transformative journey of discovering your authentic essence and nurturing a deep sense of love, compassion, and acceptance for yourself. When you recognize your inherent worth and cultivate self-love, you tap into a limitless reservoir of inner strength and empowerment. Here's how self-love becomes the cornerstone of your inner power:

Recognizing Your Inherent Worth: Self-love begins with acknowledging that you are inherently worthy, simply by being alive. Embrace the truth that you are deserving of love, happiness, and fulfillment. Release self-doubt and self-criticism, and open your heart to unconditional love for yourself.

Embracing Your Unique Self: Embrace your uniqueness and individuality. Allow yourself to be authentic and true to who you are, free from the need to conform to external expectations. Celebrate your strengths and embrace your imperfections as valuable parts of your journey.

Cultivating Self-Compassion: Treat yourself with the same compassion and kindness you would offer to a beloved friend. Embrace self-compassion in times of difficulty and vulnerability. Be gentle with yourself and understand that you are worthy of love and understanding, no matter the circumstances.

Empowering Boundaries: Self-love empowers you to set healthy boundaries that protect your well-being and honor your needs. Establishing boundaries is an act of self-respect, allowing you to prioritize your emotional and mental health.

Building Emotional Resilience: Nurturing self-love strengthens your emotional resilience. When you love and accept yourself, you develop the capacity to face challenges and bounce back from adversity with greater ease and grace.

Letting Go of Comparison: Release the habit of comparing yourself to others. Embrace your unique path and appreciate your own journey without measuring your worth against external standards. Self-love liberates you from the trap of comparison.

Fostering Positive Self-Talk: Replace self-criticism with positive self-talk. Speak to yourself with words of encouragement, support, and affirmation. Positive self-talk nurtures a mindset of self-belief and confidence.

Engaging in Self-Care: Prioritize self-care as an act of love towards yourself. Make time for activities that nourish your body, mind, and soul. Self-care replenishes your energy and strengthens your connection with your inner power.

Trusting Your Intuition: Self-love empowers you to trust your intuition and inner wisdom. Listen to the whispers of your heart and follow the guidance that arises from a place of self-love and authenticity.

Embracing Your Potential: When you love and believe in yourself, you unlock your true potential. Embrace your dreams, passions, and aspirations, knowing that you have the power within to turn them into reality.

Embracing self-love as the foundation of inner power is an empowering journey that allows you to step into your full potential and live a life of purpose, joy, and fulfillment. As you cultivate self-love, you become a radiant source of positive energy, inspiring others to embrace their own inner power. This transformative connection empowers you to live authentically, aligned with your values and true essence, and radiate love and compassion to the world around you.

- *Cultivating self-acceptance and embracing your inherent worth*

Cultivating self-acceptance and embracing your inherent worth is a profound journey of self-discovery and transformation. When you practice self-acceptance, you cultivate a deep sense of love and respect for yourself, acknowledging that you are inherently valuable and deserving of love and compassion. Here's how to embark on this transformative path:

Embrace Imperfections: Recognize that being human means having imperfections and making mistakes. Embrace your flaws and perceived shortcomings as a natural part of the human experience. Instead of judging yourself harshly, treat yourself with kindness and understanding.

Release Self-Judgment: Let go of self-judgment and negative self-talk. Replace self-criticism with self-compassion. Be gentle with yourself and speak to yourself as you would to a dear friend. Treat yourself with love and understanding, especially during challenging times.

Celebrate Your Uniqueness: Embrace your uniqueness and individuality. Celebrate your strengths, talents, and the qualities that make you who you are. You have a unique combination of traits that contribute to the richness of your being.

Practice Mindfulness: Cultivate mindfulness to become more aware of your thoughts and feelings without judgment. Observe any self-limiting beliefs or negative patterns, and gently redirect your focus towards self-acceptance and self-love.

Release Comparison: Let go of comparing yourself to others. Each person's journey is unique, and comparing yourself to others only undermines your sense of self-worth. Embrace your own path and celebrate your progress and growth.

Focus on Inner Values: Shift your focus from external validation to internal values. Recognize that your worth is not determined by external achievements or the approval of others. Cultivate a sense of self-worth that comes from living in alignment with your values and authenticity.

Practice Gratitude: Cultivate gratitude for yourself and your journey. Acknowledge the experiences and challenges that have shaped you into the person you are today. Appreciate the growth and learning that comes from embracing your inherent worth.

Forgive Yourself: Release past regrets and forgive yourself for any mistakes or choices that you regret. Understand that you are human, and making mistakes is part of the learning process. Forgive yourself and move forward with self-compassion.

Seek Support: Seek support from friends, family, or a therapist who can help you on your journey of self-acceptance. Talking openly about your feelings and experiences can be incredibly healing and validating.

Affirmations and Affection: Use affirmations and self-affectionate practices to reinforce self-acceptance. Regularly affirm your worth and repeat positive statements that resonate with you. Engage in self-care practices that demonstrate love and appreciation for yourself.

Cultivating self-acceptance and embracing your inherent worth is a transformative journey that empowers you to live authentically and joyfully. As you embrace your true self with love and compassion, you radiate a profound sense of worthiness and authenticity to the world around you. This transformative connection empowers you to step into your true power and lead a life that reflects your inherent worth and unique essence.

Chapter 10

Integrating Inner Power into Daily Life

In this final chapter, we explore the practical application of harnessing your inner power and infusing it into every aspect of your daily life. Integrating inner power is about living authentically, aligning with your values, and making conscious choices that reflect your true essence. Here's how to bring your inner power into your daily life:

Self-Awareness: Cultivate self-awareness to recognize moments when you feel empowered and when you may be giving away your power. Pay attention to your thoughts, emotions, and reactions, allowing you to respond from a place of inner strength and authenticity.

Setting Intentions: Start each day with clear intentions that align with your inner power. Set positive and empowering intentions for how you want to show up in the world and the energy you wish to embody.

Mindful Choices: Make conscious choices that reflect your values and inner power. Consider how your actions align with your authentic self and choose paths that honor your worth and purpose.

Embracing Challenges: Embrace challenges as opportunities for growth and empowerment. Approach obstacles with resilience, knowing that you have the inner strength to overcome them.

Relationships: Nurture healthy and empowering relationships that support your growth and authenticity. Set boundaries when needed and surround yourself with people who uplift and inspire you.

Career and Purpose: Align your career and life purpose with your inner power. Choose a path that resonates with your passions and values, allowing your work to be an expression of your authentic self.

Self-Care: Prioritize self-care as an act of self-love and empowerment. Make time for activities that nourish your body, mind, and soul, fostering a deeper connection with your inner power.

Mindfulness in Communication: Be mindful of your words and how you communicate with others. Speak from a place of respect, compassion, and assertiveness, staying true to your values and authentic self.

Letting Go: Release what no longer serves you, whether it be negative self-beliefs, limiting habits, or toxic relationships. Letting go creates space for your inner power to flourish.

Gratitude and Celebration: Celebrate your achievements and the progress you make on your journey. Practice gratitude for the abundance of your life, acknowledging the blessings that come from embracing your inner power.

Empowering Habits: Develop empowering habits that reinforce your inner power, such as journaling, affirmations, meditation, or acts of kindness toward yourself and others.

Embracing Change: Embrace change as a natural part of life's evolution. Your inner power allows you to adapt, grow, and navigate transitions with grace and strength.

By integrating inner power into your daily life, you cultivate a life of authenticity, purpose, and fulfillment. The journey of embracing your inner power becomes an ongoing process of self-discovery and growth. As you embody your inner strength, you radiate a profound sense of confidence and authenticity, inspiring others to do the same. This transformative connection empowers you to create a life that reflects your true essence and contributes positively to the world around you.

- *Applying the principles of inner power to relationships, career, and personal growth*

Applying the principles of inner power to relationships, career, and personal growth is a transformative process that allows you to navigate these areas of life with authenticity, confidence, and purpose. Here's how you can integrate inner power into these aspects of your life:

Relationships:

Boundaries: Set clear and healthy boundaries in your relationships, honoring your needs and respecting the needs of others. Embrace assertiveness while being compassionate.

Communication: Communicate openly and honestly, expressing your thoughts and feelings with authenticity and respect. Listen actively to understand others' perspectives.

Empathy: Cultivate empathy and understanding towards others, recognizing the shared human experience. Empathy strengthens your connections and fosters a sense of compassion in relationships.

Letting Go of Toxicity: Release toxic relationships that drain your energy and self-worth. Embrace relationships that uplift and support your growth.

Self-Love and Interdependence: Nurture self-love and embrace interdependence in relationships. Recognize that while you are whole and complete on your own, connections with others enrich your life journey.

Career:

Purpose Alignment: Align your career choices with your values and passions. Seek opportunities that resonate with your sense of purpose and empower you to make a positive impact.

Confidence in Skills: Recognize and embrace your strengths and skills. Have confidence in your abilities and leverage them to excel in your chosen career path.

Embracing Challenges: Approach challenges in your career as opportunities for growth and learning.

Embrace resilience and the belief in your capacity to overcome obstacles.

Leadership from Within: If you hold a leadership role, lead with authenticity, compassion, and integrity. Empower and inspire others by being an example of inner strength and empowerment.

Personal Growth:

Self-Reflection: Engage in regular self-reflection to understand your thoughts, emotions, and behaviors. Use self-reflection as a tool for personal growth and self-awareness.

Embracing Change: Embrace change as a natural part of life's journey. See change as an opportunity for growth and a chance to align with your evolving sense of self.

Continuous Learning: Cultivate a mindset of continuous learning and curiosity. Be open to new experiences and knowledge that expand your horizons.

Self-Development Practices: Incorporate self-development practices into your routine, such as meditation, mindfulness, or journaling, to foster inner growth and empowerment.

By applying the principles of inner power to relationships, career, and personal growth, you create a life that reflects your authentic self. Embracing your inner power allows you to approach these areas with confidence, compassion, and purpose. As you grow and embody your inner strength, you inspire those around you to do the same. This transformative connection empowers you to lead a life that aligns with your values, passions, and true essence, contributing to your personal fulfillment and the well-being of the world around you.

- *Embracing a lifestyle that reflects your inner power and authenticity*

Embracing a lifestyle that reflects your inner power and authenticity is a liberating and transformative journey of aligning your actions, choices, and values with your true essence. By living authentically, you empower yourself to embrace your unique path, make conscious decisions, and radiate the brilliance of your inner power. Here's how to embrace such a lifestyle:

Self-Reflection: Engage in regular self-reflection to understand your desires, values, and aspirations. Take time to explore what truly matters to you and align your lifestyle with your authentic self.

Letting Go of External Expectations: Release the need to conform to external expectations or societal norms. Embrace your individuality and make choices that resonate with your heart rather than seeking approval from others.

Authenticity in Relationships: Surround yourself with people who appreciate and support your authentic self. Nurture relationships that allow you to be genuine and vulnerable without fear of judgment.

Mindful Living: Practice mindfulness in your daily life. Be present and aware of your thoughts, feelings, and actions. Mindful living fosters a deeper connection with your inner power and authenticity.

Honoring Your Passions: Pursue your passions and interests wholeheartedly. Whether it's a hobby, creative pursuit, or cause you care about, dedicating time to your passions enriches your life and empowers your authentic self.

Simplifying Your Life: Consider simplifying your life by decluttering, both physically and emotionally.

Simplification creates space for what truly matters and allows your inner power to shine.

Embracing Growth and Change: Embrace personal growth and view change as a natural part of life. Embracing growth and change enables you to evolve authentically and adapt to new experiences.

Practicing Self-Care: Prioritize self-care as an act of self-love and empowerment. Take care of your physical, emotional, and mental well-being to nurture your inner power.

Setting Intentions: Set intentions that align with your inner power and authenticity. Clarify what you want to manifest in your life and infuse it with positive energy and purpose.

Trusting Your Intuition: Trust your intuition and inner guidance. Your inner power often speaks to you through intuition, leading you towards choices that resonate with your true self.

Living in Alignment with Values: Align your actions with your values. Live in integrity by making choices that reflect what you truly believe in and stand for.

Embracing Imperfection: Embrace imperfection as a beautiful part of being human. Release the need for perfection and allow yourself to be flawed, knowing that imperfections are part of your unique journey.

Embracing a lifestyle that reflects your inner power and authenticity is an empowering choice that leads to a life of fulfillment, joy, and purpose. As you live authentically, you inspire others to do the same, creating a ripple effect of positive transformation in the world. This transformative connection empowers you to lead a life that is in alignment with your true self, enabling you to contribute your unique gifts and make a meaningful impact on the world around you.

Conclusion

Embracing Your Cosmic Potential

In conclusion, embracing your cosmic potential is about recognizing your inherent worth, cultivating self-love, and aligning with the universal flow. By integrating your inner power into daily life, relationships, career, and personal growth, you unleash your unique gifts and talents. Trusting your intuition and accessing divine guidance, you become a powerful co-creator in manifesting your desires. Embracing self-love and acceptance lays the foundation for a fulfilling and authentic life. As you live authentically and align with your true essence, you tap into your boundless potential and become a radiant force for positive change in the world. Embrace your cosmic potential, for you are a magnificent being with the power to create a life of purpose, joy, and limitless possibilities.

www.ingramcontent.com/pod-product-compliance
Lightning Source LLC
Chambersburg PA
CBHW071218130726
47998CB00002B/772